People of the Bible

The Bible through stories and pictures

Joseph and the Famine

Copyright © in this format Belitha Press Ltd., 1985

Text copyright © Catherine Storr 1985

Illustrations copyright © Chris Molan 1985

Art Director: Treld Bicknell

First published in the United States of America 1985
by Raintree Publishers Inc.
310 West Wisconsin Avenue, Milwaukee, Wisconsin 53203
in association with Belitha Press Ltd., London.

Conceived, designed and produced by Belitha Press Ltd.,
2 Beresford Terrace, London N5 2DH

ISBN 0-8172-2038-0 (U.S.A.)

Library of Congress Cataloging in Publication Data

Storr, Catherine.
    Joseph and the famine.

    (People of the Bible)
    Summary: When a famine forces Joseph's brothers
to travel to Egypt to buy grain, they are reunited
with Joseph, whom they had sold into slavery.
        1. Joseph (Son of Jacob)—Juvenile literature.
2. Bible. O.T.—Biography—Juvenile literature.
[1. Joseph (Son of Jacob)   2. Bible stories—O.T.]
I. Title.   II. Series.
BS580.J6S76   1985   222′.1109505   85-12283

ISBN 0-8172-2038-0

First published in Great Britain in hardback 1985
by Franklin Watts Ltd,
12a Golden Square, London W1R 4BA

Printed in The United States of America.

 45678910111213   97 96 95 94 93 92 91 90 89 88

Joseph and the Famine

Retold by Catherine Storr
Pictures by Chris Molan

Raintree Childrens Books
Milwaukee
Belitha Press Limited • London

When Joseph was a boy, he had been sold by his brothers to merchants, who took him down to Egypt as a slave.

He grew into a wise and clever man and Pharaoh, the King, made him governor of all Egypt.

There came many years of bad harvests and there was famine in Egypt and the nearby countries.

Clever Joseph had saved enough grain from the good harvests of the years before to make sure that no one in Egypt had to go hungry. Many people from far away came to Egypt to buy corn for their starving families and animals.

In Canaan, Jacob, the father of Joseph, said
to his sons, "You will have to go to Egypt and
buy some corn so that we may stay alive."

Ten of Jacob's sons were to go down to
Egypt, but he would not let his youngest son,
Benjamin, go with the others. He had always
loved his youngest sons, Joseph and Benjamin,
best. He believed that Joseph was dead, and he
did not want to risk losing Benjamin, too.

When the ten brothers reached Egypt, they were brought before Joseph, who was the keeper of Pharaoh's storehouses. Joseph knew his brothers as soon as he saw them, but they did not recognize him. So that they would not guess who he was, he spoke roughly to them, and said, "You haven't really come to buy corn. You are spies."

9

The brothers said, "No, my lord, we twelve brothers are the sons of a man in Canaan, and we have come to buy food. One brother is dead, and one, the youngest, has stayed behind with our father."

Joseph said, "One of you must stay here as my hostage. The others may take corn back to your home. But you must bring your young brother back here, or I shall know that you haven't told me the truth."

The brothers said to each other, "We behaved badly to our brother Joseph all those years ago. Now we are being punished for what we did."

They did not know that Joseph could understand what they were saying, because he pretended not to know their language.

But he heard them speaking of their cruelty to him when he was a boy. They had thrown him into a pit and then sold him as a slave.

He went away and wept.

Joseph kept one brother, Simeon, as his
prisoner. He told his servants to fill each
brother's sack with corn, and on top of the
corn to put the money that brother had paid
for it.

The brothers started on their journey back to Canaan. On the way, one of them opened his sack so that he could feed his ass. He saw the money he had paid to Joseph, and he was afraid. The brothers said to each other, "What has God done to us?"

When the brothers reached their home, they found that each brother had been given back his money. They told Jacob, their father, what had happened, and that the Egyptian lord had told them that they must bring their youngest brother back with them to Egypt.

Jacob said, "You are robbing me of my children. My son Joseph is dead, and Simeon is left in Egypt. Now you want to take Benjamin from me, too. You will bring my grey hairs with sorrow to the grave."

Reuben said, "I promise to bring Benjamin back safely. If I don't, you may kill my two sons."

The famine grew worse and worse. At last, Jacob said to his sons, "You will have to go back to Egypt to buy more corn."

Judah said, "We can't go back without Benjamin. The Egyptian lord said he would not see us again if we did not bring our youngest brother with us."

Jacob said, "Why did you tell the lord that you had another brother?"

His sons said, "He asked us about our family, if our father was still alive, and if we had another brother. We promise we will bring Benjamin back safely."

At last Jacob agreed to let Benjamin go to
Egypt. He said, "Take a present to this lord.
Take some of the best fruit we have, and take
balm and honey and spices and myrrh and
nuts and almonds. Take double the money with you.

It must have been a mistake last time that you found your money in your sacks of corn."

The brothers took the money and the fruit and the spices, and, with Benjamin, they went down to Egypt.

When Joseph saw them, he said to his servants, "Prepare a meal. These men shall eat with me."

The brothers were brought to Joseph's house, but they were afraid. They said to each other, "He is going to punish us for taking the money that we found in our sacks."

They told Joseph's servant how they had discovered the money and said, "We have brought back double the money this time."

The servant said, "Don't be afraid. God must have given you the money in your sacks. I have the money you paid me for the corn."

The brothers came into Joseph's house. When they saw Joseph, they bowed down to him. He asked, "How is your father? Is he still alive?" Then Joseph saw Benjamin and asked, "Is this the young brother that you told me about?" To Benjamin he said, "God be gracious to you."

But he had to go away quickly to his own room to weep alone. Joseph washed his face. Then he composed himself and went out to the feast he had prepared for his brothers.

He put food in front of each brother. But he gave Benjamin five times as much as to any of the others.

After the feast, Joseph told his
servants to fill the brothers' sacks
with food, and to put each man's
money into the sack, too. "Put my
silver cup into Benjamin's sack,"
he said.

When the morning was light,
the brothers went on their way.

Then Joseph sent a servant after them, to say that they had returned evil for good, because they had stolen from Joseph's house.

The brothers said, "We have stolen nothing. Look in our sacks. If you find anything, in any man's sack, let him die."

The servant searched the brothers' sacks, and he found the silver cup in Benjamin's sack. The brothers were terrified. They tore their clothes to show their misery, and they returned with the servant to the city.

When they came to Joseph's house, they fell down before him, and Judah said, "What can we say to you? We will be your servants to make up for this terrible thing."

Joseph said, "I will keep the man who stole my cup."

But Judah said, "Our father is an old man. He did not want Benjamin to come down to Egypt. Take me as your servant instead of him. If he does not return, our father will certainly die."

Then Joseph could not keep his secret any longer, and he wept aloud. He said to his brothers, "I am Joseph, your brother, whom you sold into Egypt when I was a boy. Go and tell my father that God has made me lord of all Egypt. Tell my father to bring his household, his servants, and his cattle down here to live with me."

The brothers went back to Canaan, carrying meat and corn and bread. When Jacob heard their story, he said, "Joseph my son is alive. I will go and see him before I die."

Joseph went out of the city to greet his father, and when they met, they embraced and wept for joy.

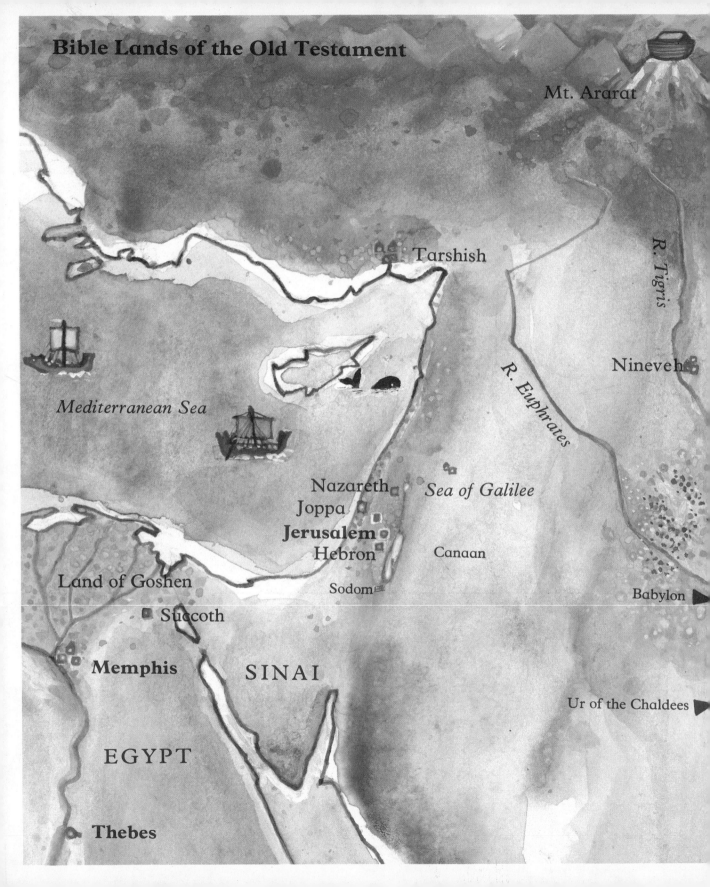